The Lady In My Head

Poetry and Healing Thoughts

Jamie Gelner

Made with ❤ on the BookLeaf Publishing Platform
www.bookleafpub.in
www.bookleafpub.com

Dedication

Thank you to my husband Jon for believing in me when I couldn't believe in myself.

Preface

This collection of poetry contains my early writings. I did not set out to write a poetry book, however, writing became a part of my healing journey. It has allowed me to express bottled up trauma that I did not have the courage to say out loud.

Thank you for reading.

Acknowledgements

Special thanks to Tess Guinery for teaching me how beautiful poetry is through her writings, Anee Lamott for reminding me to take life one bird at a time, Elizabeth Gilbert for inspiring me to find my magic, Katherine May for teaching me to winter, and finally, Mel Robbins for calling me out for avoiding writing this book.

Trauma Cycle

I was born with my sky falling
my father's fell on him

he was left to have pancakes
while his mom walked up the hill

towards her new life

Nature Notes

A feather arrives just as I start
signaling this to be the right path for reflection

it is brown and red in color
with a few tips of white
damaged and frazzled

it is a beautiful sight

maybe I'm seeing myself as I mend it
taking the time to show care

I see a few flecks of something else
here and there

I see its message

Memories

Alone I sit
only Christmas lights aglow
remembering the years of

peanuts not presents

how could she?
again, and again

I now see

she sat in her spiral
only Christmas light aglow

wishing
begging
hoping
yet, knowing

Christmas morning would never be my fairy tale

I now see

I sit in a silent spiral
digging up Christmas pasts

wishing
begging
hoping
praying

I fulfill Christmas dreams

I now see

Love is all I need to give

was it there and I didn't see it?

Tired Soul

I lie in bed waiting to be reborn

sleep come find me
I'm not hiding from you

sleep come find me
before the mimic of noon

sleep come find me
I'm not hiding from you

You are not Alone

What pain have you suffered that made you so pleasing?

what pain have you suffered that made you so hateful?

what pain have you suffered, dear friend?

I can listen

Abused Friend

I am a magnet to the suffering

I want to help you

I do

I can't

I couldn't help my mom
and I can't help you

help yourself

leave

Remorse

I wake up crying
not knowing who I am

not wanting to go
not wanting to do
not wanting to feel pain

not wanting to be the me
I have become

Spiral

It's always the hope of the next day

the thought of a new beginning
allowing me to drift to sleep

maybe tomorrow I will get a sign
maybe tomorrow I won't cry

I will look in the mirror and smile instead of frown
my clothes won't feel tight or look wrong
an extra grey hair will not create a spiral down
a check of social media won't make me chase my
shadow

I don't know how many more days I can wake up

just to cry all over again

Advice

Do as I say
not as I do

I told myself I am ugly
I am stupid
I am vain

I am fat
I am lucky to be liked

I am annoying
I am too emotional

I did what you wanted
I repeated what you said

repeated your thoughts
your words

and now I hate myself
just like you

Punished

Pain
a turn on to others

tears
ignite their flame

hiding
makes them search

I can't be alone

they are always here
to tell me my flaws

Old Soul

I am born of many lifetimes

I hold too much pain for just one

its depths do not end

absent is a break for my fall

I call out to my shadow

I don't want it to be scared

I want it to play

you can find yourself

I say

A Wish

There is a lady that dances in my head sometimes
I don't know where she is

she stays away too long

when she is there, she is free

free to speak without stuttering
walk without freezing
sing without care

her hair is untamed
her tattoos uncovered

she walks without shame or guilt
yet, her flaws are not hidden

there is a lady that dances in my head sometimes
I don't know where she lives

she stays away too long

is she my past?
should she be my present?
or is she a promise to be?

she is not supported by structure
she floats without fear
she is playful and at peace

I long to find her

she stays away too long

there is a lady that dances in my head sometimes
she and I are me

Soul Mate

Today I sit
alone in the woods

I've discovered my father's shadow has driven my past
leaving me to wonder what choices were truly mine

is my life mine?
is my life untrue?

how can I justify keeping you?

my shadow will always appear
whispering our relationship is false

did my shadow choose you?
or was it my soul?

my mind talks in circles
convincing me you are a mirage
a dream

hallucination

a pure wish
that we are one

Change

The paths I have been walking are worn

tattered
boring
predictable

they have been walked and repeated

walked and repeated

Messages

The universe talks to me

it sends me feathers to decipher
whispers to hear

the universe leaves me wondering

why do brown leaves always fall
they feel of death

the universe leaves me hopeful
it sends me signs
leaving me to search for answers

I can be found combing the paths I walk

searching for feathers
sitting in the trees
feeling the whispers in the wind

Afraid to Live

Overtime my spirit has become fearful
fearful of this world

I am afraid when I wake
afraid to be myself

I live in shame

afraid to sing
someone will hear

terrified to talk
they won't feel what I feel

scared to taste life
new things threaten

I have turned up my nose to living
suspicion is always wafting near

Waiting

I lie on my back
spreading out wide like a snow angel

frozen in fear and pain

soaking up the sun in hope of healing

I lie here frozen on my wooden bridge

stuck in my life labyrinth
numb to my core

even the vultures think I am dead

Escape

I want to run
run from myself

anger pours out of my mouth
like a swarm of bees

I leave it hanging open wide
hoping this is the last time

the last time I am angry
the last time I am so sad
the last time I can't function

why can't I follow through?

I know better
I am out of control

unstoppable
unsolvable

maybe I should vanish
to save my family from my pain

unknowingly
it has been made theirs

I want to run
run from myself

In-between

I seek
less is seen

I share
my words feel unheard

emotions flare

I sense my shadow near
awaiting answers

I fight self-sabotage
and lying whispers

My Soul

Twisting
winding
bending
steep

unpredictable
frightful
surprising
seen

calm
relaxed
awaiting

not a dead end

under construction

Lost

Please Mother Earth
warm my soul
blow me in the right direction
wash my sorrows away

I am listening
I am feeling
I will obey

I am you
you are me
we are one

please Mother Earth
tell me your secrets
and whisper mine too

www.ingramcontent.com/pod-product-compliance
Lightning Source LLC
LaVergne TN
LVHW021333200726
843509LV00014B/2520